JURISPRUDENCE

of

GOOD AND RIGHT

A Treatise on Juridical Activism and Fiat

CHARLES MWEWA

Copyright © 2024 Charles Mwewa

www.charlesmwewa.com

Published by:

ACP

Ottawa, ON Canada

www.acpress.ca

www.spirngopus.com

Email:

info@acpress.ca

ISBN: 978-1-998788-80-4

DEDICATION

For Prof. Munyonzwe Hamalengwa,
for attaining to the title of,
"Professor of Law."

CONTENTS

INTRODUCTION

The question people ruminate over is whether law and God judge men's good or right. So far it seems like it is only men who judge themselves on the scale of goodness. Such judgments could not be correct or even morally acceptable.

Men's intentions and actions cannot be pegged on their goodly behavior. It can only be truly judged on the scale of right and wrong.

Even human judges, justices and jurists would not qualify to sit on benches and judge men's intentions and actions if the former were the standards. It is only because of the later that human judgment is tolerated.

At the End of this Treatise

You should be able to:

1. Recognize the distinctions between good and right
2. Ascertain the relativity of good in the process of truth-seeking and justice-making
3. Ascertain the absoluteness of right in the process of truth-seeking and justice-making
4. Explain the preference for right, and not good, in juridical decision-making

JURISPRUDENCE OF GOOD AND RIGHT

Distinction between Good and Right

Good

Good is based on an arbitrary hypothetical scale. There is no absolute recognition of good anywhere. While some things or behaviors may be determined through practice and experience to be good, it still remains so only in tandem with cultural and socially contextual perceptions and permutations.

What may be good today might be bad tomorrow and vice-versa. This is because society and culture are transitory, and are not static. They change from time to time and era to epoch. As society and culture evolve and change, so do people's tastes and preferences. Thus, helping a disabled individual from navigating a winded terrain might have been construed as good in olden times, but now it could be taken as an offence, or something bad or even impolite. This is because as society updates itself with more and equitable understanding of ableness vis-à-vis a history of bigotry and discrimination, it tends to redefine itself in terms of what it now considers good. Beliefs and attitudes, too, change, so that what was perceived as good or bad yesteryear, may be taken as good or bad presently, respectively.

Does good change? Yes, it does. But this change must be contextually assessed. Good is not universal as some may think. Good changes and what is good now may only be based on today's understanding of good. Character, though, may be a factor in the consideration of what is good and what is bad. It impedes on our sense of order to make meaningful judgments.

What does it mean when people say that God is good? It may mean that to a person who experiences the good side of God, to that individual God is good. Similarly, a person who might experience the bad side of a meal, for example, to that person the meal is bad. However, good can only be sustained by qualification. For example, in our illustration of the good side of God, it would be in order to say, "God is good always," rather than to end only at, "God is good." The qualification "always," is instructive of this thesis. It would be preposterous for anyone to confidently say, "I am good," or, even, "I am always good." Even nature would clench its fist to that ingratitude. But it is reasonable to say, that, with qualification, thus, "I am good at playing soccer," with the implied assumption of the relativity of good.

Right

Right, on the other hand, deals in absoluteness. Right is always right. It changes only with either consensus or by divine decree. Thus, law, divine or human, could deliberately change or be changed to define a structure for the purposes of reaching consensus. For example, right, to naturalist thinking, is what nature or God has said or declared to be right. In other words, consistency is proof, and as long as nature continues to reinforce certain happenstances as right, then they are right. There is a sense of finality, a sense of consistency to them.

In realistic thinking, on the other hand, right is what the recognized sovereign says it is. In passing laws, parliamentary fiat is the constructed consensus. Thus, even if the law may be bluntly bad or even discriminatory, in parliamentary parlance, it still remains right and must be observed and obeyed. Subjects cannot question it or disregard it, except on their own peril. The idea is that, the law was reached or made, or otherwise enacted, by majority consensus, and majority vetting wins over individual interests.

So, right is universal only in the sense that it is divinely ordained or ordered or nature has an imprint on it, or it was reached by consensus and consent. Otherwise, right is the idealization of good over a long period of time. The inference is that what is good for a long period of time, ends up becoming right.

Can right change? Over a very long period of time, yes. But right cannot change without systematic ramifications. In other words, what changes is, in fact, systems themselves and not right itself. Thus, a law may be amended or repealed to contextualize it in a particular system.

It may not be the principle of law itself that changed, but the system in which that principle operated.

For example, the legal definition of marriage in Canada used to be a legal union between a man and a woman. The system changed and men vied to marry men and women, women. The law had to be adapted to the changing regime, to, thus, define marriage, at least in Canada, as the union between men and women, men and men and women and women. The idea of *union* itself remains. However, the applicability of that conception had to change to accommodate new realities such as the "rights" of the homosexuals.

To conservative point of view, change is unnatural because it goes against the consistency of nature. However, liberals may view change as the order of, ironically, nature itself. That it changes to accommodate new thoughts, new ideas, new trends and new systems. Change is, thus, a necessity of life because it aids in the amelioration of historical or human wrongs. Change is right, by liberal-realistic thinking.

So, what is at issue, in both naturalistic and realistic parlance, is not right itself, but the ambit of justice vis-à-vis truth. To naturalists, right is the instrument. They justify it by reference to divine actions. Thus, law must be morally endearing to be law. Law must not offend divine order, and right is what the divine say is right. And it must be obeyed no matter what is at stake.

So, if a man realizes that he may only have affinity for other men, in naturalistic and conservative thinking, that kind of orientation is wrong because it is not right. That man must ignore the plight of human imagination and embrace the resolute endearment to the law of nature and to God.

Similarly, to naturalist philosophy, abortion is murder, no matter the justification or what is at stake. The right ambiance is amplified in this theorization. Because nature is above the law and must inform the application of its salient principles in human affairs.

However, if right is the gist, then wrong is deliberately silenced to mute conscience. Justice may be silenced, too. Because the question of justice is silenced, then to what end is right? For example, in saving the life of the mother, the child might die. Or in saving the life of a child, the mother might die. In these so-called moral dilemmas, what is at stake, in fact, may not even be right, truth or justice; it may, and conceptually so, be duty. It would appear that only duty is at play and neither justice nor truth avail much. For if the child dies, and the mother lives, and vice-versa, one is wronged and an injustice has been done. Any action will have adverse moral effects on the other. Naturalists, thus, will argue that natural or divine order must take preeminence and that is sufficient.

That still does not answer the question whether nature or God's moral demands are devoid of justice and right. The rational answer seems to be no. However, excusing such actions, or lack of actions, on nature or God's moral demands would maim the very premise on which right is based.

In historical times, God Himself had allowed the humans to implement deeds that might not be construed as right. For example, it may be argued that part of the human race originated from an incestuous arrangement in which Noah's daughters had to sire children for their father by hoodwinking Noah into sexual relations. God would have allowed that to sustain a lineage. Similarly, God had to change the entire Old Testament system with its sacrifices and liturgies to bring in a New Testament system by means of grace. In both of these cases, right still remained constant, subtly. However, truth and justice seemed to have been at issue.

It was, indeed, wrong for daughters to have intercourse with their father. But it was right for the sake of generational perpetuity. It is, indeed, wrong for those who died under the Old Covenant, under the law. But it was right for the heirs of salvation by grace through faith in Christ Jesus. The point is that a wrong was always righted by a right. This, too, begs to reiterate the issues raised earlier, namely, does right change, or in a layman's language, does right end up becoming wrong? Implicitly, it seems unchallenged, even by mere conscience, that right cannot be wrong. Right is right because it is right. But from the illustrations of Noah and the covenantal replacements, it seems cogent that what may be seen as wrong could also serve a right purpose. Therefore, right still remains constant – because even when a wrong is being *righted*, it is being righted for the purposes of bringing it into the right column. It would seem, too, that the process of *righting* a wrong is righteousness towards God but deleterious towards men.

This would fall well into naturalistic sentimentalities. That God and nature cannot be questioned; what must be questioned are human motives. Thus, an abortion is wrong because God or nature says or implies it to be wrong, no matter the circumstance or justification. And similarly, a man must not engage in sexual relations with another man because that would go against the grain of nature and of God. In these illustrations, right is preserved because God and nature are honored. This is at the heart of conservative, naturalistic thinking.

However, what is being swept under the carpet, are issues of truth and justice. God and nature may not be questioned, granted. But liberal and realistic thought might argue that in the pursuit of right, truth and justice might be sacrificed. This would not be far from realism in the sense that the will of the sovereign dictates what is right and wrong at the expense of justice and truth. Both schools of thought entertain this gaping dilemma.

In politics, it is commonly asserted that Hitler did not trifle with parliamentary process because he only implemented the laws it passed, however draconian and discriminatory. Those laws indiscriminately indicted Blacks and Jews and even subjected them to untold historic and human atrocities in gas chambers, the holocaust. In this respect, realism's parity of argument is that the massacres of millions of Jews and Blacks would be justified under these permutations. And, indeed, it should if only the requirements of the constitution are to carry out the duties of law. In short, for Hitler not to implement the holocaustic laws would be "wrong" because they were the dictates of legitimate sovereign action. In other words, they were "acts" of parliament. Implicitly, too, the argument, at least under this view, is sustained if we consider the alternative. And that alternative would be for Hitler to dismiss the requirements of constitutional fiat and refuse to implement the draconian laws passed by his parliament.

Naturalists would agree with this move, but realists would disagree. For naturalism, laws can either be "good" or "bad," but never right or wrong, interestingly. Thus, laws that give women the right to abortion may be bad laws under conservatism, but laws that take away that right could be right. For liberals, laws that allow women to marry their fellow women might be right, but those that take away that right could be wrong.

This brings into question the entire review of right and wrong under both regimes. Indeed, right, whether severing from nature or naturalistic in nature, is right. Both naturalists and realists at the end of the day claim to be in the pursuit of right. What seems to be at issue is their methods.

But can it be said that law can be wrong depending on who it impacts? And the obvious and initial answer may seem to be yes, given the inimicality of discriminatory laws. If this stands, the entire premise of the absoluteness and universality of right falls. For then right cannot always be right. And the unstated inference is that in certain circumstances, right can be wrong. If this last statement stands, then it must also be true that morality may not be absolute.

And this line of thinking may open up a pandora box of all sorts of possibilities and conclusions. For example, it could be true that when a judge sentences a convicted criminal to death, it could be patently wrong because a judge is humanly limited to knowing and judging the true intentions of men. The judge may make the ruling based on precedent and juridical discretion, however, in the process, she might do injury to her own conscience. In this scenario, the question of right still emerges, was the judge right to sentence an offender to death? Wouldn't a life sentence suffice if justice's own limitations are factored in?

And this now brings us to the whole idea of right verse justice. Should a judge who has discovered the truth or who believes that truth has been established by the proffered evidence condemn the convicted criminal to harsher penalty or sentence? What will be the purported achievement or purpose in that? To change behavior, for deterrence, or punishment, perhaps? There could only be one of the two reasons – either for right or justice.

Right – in the context of truth, stands on its own. What is right is inherently truthful. But justice has to meet a comparative standard. It is just because if not pursued, another suffers as a result. Justice is always relative to truth; it cannot stand on its own. Thus, a judge is under compulsion to mete out truth with justice as a balancing scepter, or even as a vindictive excuse. The punitive action taken against the convicted criminal, to whatever level, must meet the proportionality test – in an attempt to bring balance of a general consensus that wrong must always be punished. That is the province of justice. It cries out for balance, for equilibrium using the instrument of truth.

Right, on the other hand, seems to be a stand-alone proposition. It may not bow, even to justice. It may not be relative to truth, either. Right remains right even in the presence of truth. It is neither affected nor modified by truth. It changes no state to accommodate or acclimatize to prevailing conditionalities. Thus, a judge who with the presentation of evidentiary truth and who finds that it is just to sentence a convicted felon to a harsher punishment, may still be amenable to the veracity of right and be lenient. The judge's coming to this conclusion, to exercise her natural instinct to be and to do right, is unaffected by the material circumstances.

However, because social orientation is suspect to such conclusions, it might lead to unintended assumptions. One of such assumptions may be that there could be suspicion of corruption, and even of injustice. So, intentionally, jurists may have to lend themselves to justifications. These justifications may variously be termed, "reasons for the decision," *ratio decidendi*, etc. Jurists, judges and justices must, thus, explain their judgments even when they have a right to exercise their judicial immunities. The reason is a matter of conscience more than of law. Hitherto, only God retains the power to simply action right without any justification, at least, in practice.

The naturalists may find this last statement a dialectical conundrum. In one, they must insist that only God is right; in the other, they must require justices to explain their judgments. Thus, they may know the truth but they may be more compelled to avow to right than to the truth. Taking the case of abortion as an example. Where the life of the mother is at stake, naturalists will be more likely to assert right and ignore the truth. Indeed, it is right not to kill, but, in this specific case, it might be wrong not to kill to preserve another life. Either way, two lives are at stake (the unformed or not fully formed one in the form of a fetus; and the mother's). What may be right in one, would be wrong in the other – because both involve the sanctity of life. Thus, for naturalists, truth may be trifled at the expense of right. The assumption of *trite law*, too, falls apart in this gesture. For what is trite is premised on consensus, and not truth. And consensus is within the province of right, and not truth.

The same quandary applies to the realists, but in the opposite way. Truth is asserted but right is compromised. Given an extreme example of an employer who must hire a homosexual person because the law requires him to do so, but his moral or social predispositions are anti-homosexual predilections. A naturalists may be afflicted by his conscience, but a realist may not.

A naturalist might, thus, refuse to assert the right at the expense of truth, and through that act of refusal, he might incur the wrath of the law, suffering the consequences of vetting right and ignoring truth. In the eyes of general consensus, he has subverted the law. However, his conscience may move him to side with right. The realist has no such predilections – because to the realist, truth and right are what the sovereign say they are. To a realist, both abortions to prevent the death of the fetus or of the mother, are not a matter of conscience but of practicality. And to hiring the homosexuals, a realist may entertain no qualms as to his conscience, in accepting the homosexual employee, he has asserted both right and truth. His conscience is at rest.

In all cases, given justice, truth and right, whether adducing this from naturalistic or realistic convictions, it is only right that remains constant. Truth and justice are only variables that may be instrumentalized or weaponized to meet particular ends. As a result, right triumphs over truth and justice, just like mercy does so over judgment.

Good verses Right

The underlying principle may be stated, thus, good is relative and right is absolute. The universality of right and the relativity of good, may help to understand why even in extreme situations, conscience may emerge the winner.

Good may be superior to bad, but it is demoted by right. Conscience does not conform to good but only to right. And that seems to be an innate quality all living beings possess. When living things are given a choice, they all tend to defend right rather than good. As an example, even a cruel master would be compelled to defend his slave, not because it is good (profit), but because he deems it right (conscience). Sometimes, it is both, for profit and conscience, however, even in that duality of action, he prefocuses the ounce of human compunction leaning heavily towards right.

Similarly, even die-hard racists would save a human life that they have no racial regard for and not an animal given a dialectical choice or dilemma. More women who give birth to the so-called "unwanted" children, choose to leave them at orphanages than throwing them away to marauding wildernesses. Even in war, soldiers need a more convincing or compelling reason to shoot and kill than simply killing for sport or vengeance. At the heart of these benevolent ostentations is right, and not mere good. They feel, believe and know that it is right. And, so, it is not just good to do right, but more so right to do good.

On October 7th, 2023, Hamas brutally massacred Israelis and kidnapped men, women and children. Israel reiterated. But it was barely a few days after the fact when Isarel had levelled most of northern Palestine that the global citizenry rose in condemnation of Israel. The United

Nations in a resolution voted against the continuation of aggression, even Canada supported it.

At issue was the question of proportionality, which is a quintessential question of right. It was *good* that Israel reiterated but it was *right* that they did so proportionately or justly. Human instincts always tilt towards right and not good. Death-bed confessions are a triage of righting wrongs, no matter how good people might have thought the deceased was. No-one in their right mind asserts their goodness before death, but only with regard to what is right. Because they know, implicitly or explicitly, that right stands a test of time and is perpetual.

Good can be taught in schools, but right is conscience-based and is durable. And all legal systems of the world premise their truth-finding investigations on right, and not good. And it is right, and not good, that gives impetus to truisms and sanctities, such as life and liberty.

Conclusion

Nature, conscience and God all bear witness to the superiority of right over good. Human nature may be inherently bad (not good), but humanity has still survived because, at the core of human nature, there is a propensity to pursuing right. Judging, thus, must be situated centrally within this ambit of right's pursuit. This, for humans, is a more trusting approach to the search for truth and the doings of justice than succumbing to the quandaries of being and establishing good. A judge who is caught in between truth and justice, must always err on the side of right, and not good.

ASSESSMENT REVIEW

1. In the light of two competing dialectics of right and good, discuss the implications:

   a) To a naturalist, of the advantage of right over good in the search for truth; and
   b) To a realist, of the disadvantage of right over good in the search for truth.

2. Of the three imperatives, right, truth and justice, which one remains constant regardless of philosophical persuasions and convictions? Justify your answer with an illustration from a judge who must make a decision on an abortion case.

3. Musa is a Muslim cleric from United Arab Emirates (UAE) who is also an ardent supporter of heterogenous, polygamous marriages. On his secondment to Canada, he must choose between accepting Canadian same-sex legislation or giving up one of his two wives because Canada does not allow polygamous marriages. What will likely be Musa's dilemma and how would he attempt to resolve it in the context of different theosophical differences on law and morality between Canada and UAE?

4. Mwengeshi is a judge of the Zambian High Court. Before him is a case of allowing a man to marry another man, because there is ample evidence to show that "the two love each other soul and body." Mwengeshi is a pragmatic realist but he finds himself in

conflict with the leanings of a predominantly Christian nation in which he is employed. What is likely to be Mwengeshi's decision and how will he justify it?

5. "Right must triumph over good, as mercy over judgment." Discuss.

6. Right, truth and justice. Situate the three on the reliability and certainty continuum, and list and explain one of the three as a durable moral quality endeared by men and gods alike.

7. Describe two scenarios in which it may be "good to do right" and "right to do good."

ABOUT THE AUTHOR

Award-Winning, Best-Selling Author, Charles Mwewa (LLB; BA Law; BA Ed; LLM), is a prolific researcher, poet, novelist, lawyer, law professor and Christian apologist and intercessor. Mwewa has written no less than 100 books and counting in every genre and has exhibited his works at prestigious expos like the Ottawa International Book Expo and is the winner of the Coppa Awards for his signature publication, *Zambia: Struggles of My People.*
Mwewa and his family live in the Canadian Capital City of Ottawa.

SELECTED BOOKS BY THIS AUTHOR

1. *ZAMBIA: Struggles of My People (First and Second Editions)*
2. *10 FINANCIAL & WEALTH ATTITUDES TO AVOID*
3. *10 STRATEGIES TO DEFEAT STRESS AND DEPRESSION: Creating an Internal Safeguard against Stress and Depression*
4. *100+ REASONS TO READ BOOKS*
5. *A CASE FOR AFRICA?S LIBERTY: The Synergistic Transformation of Africa and the West into First-World Partnerships*
6. *DECOLONIZATION: Reclaiming African Originality and Destiny*
7. *A PANDEMIC POETRY, COVID-19*
8. *ALLERGIC TO CORRUPTION: The Legacy of President Michael Sata of Zambia*
9. *BOOK ABOUT SOMETHING: On Ultimate Purpose*
10. *CAMPAIGN FOR AFRICA: A Provocative Crusade for the Economic and Humanitarian Decolonization of Africa*
11. *CHAMPIONS: Application of Common Sense and Biblical Motifs to Succeed in Both*

INDEX

www.ingramcontent.com/pod-product-compliance
Lightning Source LLC
Chambersburg PA
CBHW061239030726
47595CB00004B/1609